Man In A Crow Suit

Man In A Crow Suit
Poems
by Ray Greenblatt

Poems copyright © 2020 by Ray Greenblatt
Linocut Illustrations are © 2020 Meg Kennedy
All rights reserved
Printed in the United States of America
First Edition

Published by

BookArts Press
www.book-arts-press.com
ISBN 978-0-9795861-6-3

Table Of Contents

Introduction

This is a book of poems featuring crows. I like crows because they can symbolize so many things. Ted Hughes wrote about crows in 1970; I have amassed corvine poems over many years and now—fifty years later—publish my book. Crows still abide. Some poems—Crow's Voice, Crow Highway, Crow In The Garden—are still elusively floating around and I can't seem to locate them. However, enough poems roost in this little book to stick in your craw. Even their cousin, the raven, sneaks in.

Man In A Crow Suit

Man puts on a crow suit
and goes out on the lawn,
not much different from
hanging with old pals
at the VFW post.
Nibbling road kill is close to
a burger at McDonalds,
fast food meaning move quick
or you might be next course.
Passing trucks wouldn't
even notice until
they swerve at sight of
cigar in beak.

GATHERING

The old men met in the park
stumbling around
flapping their arms to stay warm,
mumbling to themselves
and to each other,
"Got a chaw, boy, got a chaw?"
"Old lady kicked me out
so she could clean."
"Mean weather, too damn cold!"
"Oh well, time for
a cup of corn."
"Goodbye, Mr. Crow, old pal,
see you tomorrow."

ON A BRANCH

Crow swings open the left side
of his slick plastic raincoat,
all kinds of watches hanging there—
opens right side to reveal
real Cuban cheroots.
Well, what'll it be?
he squints at me
rolls eyes upward.
And his response to my badinage?
a cackle of a laugh,
a spit in the eye
or flapping mutely
into nearby cornfield.

That Crow Is My Uncle

My Uncle Herb is
in that crow walking
around like Groucho Marx
looking up females' skirts.
Last night he thought the moon
had a nylon draped across
its face, cats' eyes peered down
at him from the sky.
Uncle Herb tries the shuffle,
he waves his hair around
like a dish rag, croaks a song
that astonishes three
ladies waiting for the bus.

Acting

Crows pick a bare willow
to play at being vultures,
their hunching so realistic.
A young crow sounds
like a kid blowing through
an empty Crackerjack box.
An older one simulates
an old woman startled
by a rap on her door.
Even in this heavy heat
they play at life, mock
everyone around and make
summer slide faster.

CROWS

The man shifted
and had one more dream—
were they shadows?
No, crows
in the rain
large and gleaming black with savvy,
coasting over harvested fields
to pick up kernels of corn
and fill their bellies with chowder.
The man clawed
stiffly to his feet,
grimy coat
flapping in the wind.

ON CROWS LAUGHING

Crows detach themselves
from tops of poplars and
flap away snickering
over their shoulder.
In middle of the day
their laughs might rise out of
middle of a cornfield—
did they know I was passing?
Guess I'm a bit like them
when cars whip by me,
seeing an odd codger
who stands there staring at what,
laughing into space.

GAMBLERS

Crows squat in winter fields
on cornstalk stumps like
they were on barstools,
"Another round of Kernel!"
They bet on anything,
long odds whether those geese
will get hit crossing the road,
but they turn into a fan
rising in time toward the clouds.
The crows guffaw at anything,
betting two-to-one black ice
will skid cars,
then a "Crash!" as they "Caw!"

MISCHIEF

A rainstorm roars through the
woods
or is it merely wind?
perfect day for mischief:
bird adjusts sooty costume,
snaps in contact lenses
of beady brightness,
pops on big orange schnoz
(he has screeched himself hoarse
last night in anticipation)
and steps forward on the branch
to impersonate crow,
having lots of fun at it
letting blame be fixed where it may.

HECKLERS

The crows have been stirred up
since the building began
appearing everywhere all day.
They have come in from the fields
to watch—more precisely
their fields are being invaded.
They wait till the dozer gets
close then flap away,
guffaw when the crane gets stuck.
Dust doesn't bother them,
they caw down engine sounds
and perch boldly on the rigging.
The workers must remember
as kids they shot crows for sport
and fingers itch again.
We've never heard so many
varied sounds the crows now make,
forming words or curses.

Breaking Ground

Crows are on
every mound of dirt,
sometimes alone or
in groups of odd numbers,
their feathers ruffling
at the slightest breeze.
Their beaks are open—
are they gasping for air,
is it the word they are passing
as they notice each
slash of the metal, each
mortared slab slide into place,
or are they setting the incantation.

To Be Announced

You crows hang in trees
like old lanterns, or swoop like
daylight vampires,
your harsh calls disguising
unceasing good humor.
Soon these cornfields, trees, barns
of which you are caretaker
will be gone, to make way
for an industrial park.
You have been here first
and will continue, I am sure,
knowing well how to adapt
better than I.

Obnoxious

Crows cruise low over us
just to be
obnoxious,
they pace off the park
first one way—then the other,
they squat like statuary
left out in the rain.
Crows call as kids do
at the height of a game
and gibber just when you try
to listen to music.
One crow slurs like a drunk
through the swinging doors.

Crows Fly Up

Crows whiz up behind
my car like cinders,
like bark off a wind-ripped pine.
A crow hurtles toward my window
burning an imprint
of danger on the glass.
They swirl around the car,
now a claustrophobic room
engulfed by dark thoughts.
I must make a decision:
turn back to things undone
or drive on into
a blinding sunset.

On A Stoplight

Crow bowing on top of
the traffic light,
flipping direction each hop,
gurgling in rhythm.
Does the amber light
remind him of corn,
green tone the fields,
red a very hot day.
Is he telling us something?
is he hexing the light?
or just jiving?
Moment light changes
he's off faster than traffic.

Gleaners

It's crow-collecting time,
it's corn-collecting time
in gray early morning fields,
fog droops over them
moisture drips over them,
they peer soulfully
down long noses as they go
about their busy work
of picking and pecking,
overcoats drab and frazzled
overshoes non-descript,
but their eyes gleam with
enduring grit.

Bare Times

Stubble in a field
is a cold carpet,
a dulled sort of brass;
no surprise, crows look
servile, beaten as they work it
for leftover kernels.
Leafless woods appear dry
like tinder about to catch,
grave faces at a memorial;
no wonder come spring
we vigorously spread
grass seed on any bare spot,
not caring if crows get a bit.

Carnivore

The hanging man does
a graceful dance in the wind,
as the crow pecks out an eye
to gain further foresight,
pries out gold fillings
to furnish his nest
the finest mansion in the tree;
crow goes about his job
with no malice save
as skilled workman
cleaning up, wasting not,
clothes to the poor and
leather to line the walks.

OVER THE PARKING LOT

Shadows whoosh over my newspaper,
a paper I should be
reading for the news.
Two crows make sounds,
harsh hoots I'm unfamiliar with,
skimming low over my car
then landing in a bare winter elm.
Such a shock I'm still feeling
shudders up my neck!
I'm here, aren't I
taking time off from essential work
to wait for her to shop
doing my good deed.
I have to catch up with what's happening
and even crows can distract me.
They pose there, quite a pair,
caught in the film of cold air,
giant oil tanks rearing up behind them.
One crow begins to bob
up and down as if
in a kind of primitive prayer.

CURSE OF THE MALL

One good thing they did was
leave a grove of chestnuts in
the middle of the mall.
But that is where crows
have lived for untold years
in dark community.
How scurrying shoppers
are denounced by cackles
crude as a gang of thugs.
Diners under canopies
at the outdoor café
wince at huge ebony shadows
zooming down and closing in.

BIRDS SWIRLING

Over the mall
a flock of birds circle
momentarily a long plume,
suddenly a black parasol;
they each grow in shadow
then double their number
against an alabaster wall
to perch on a high balustrade,
caryatids in a row;
people don't glance up,
only stare in shock at leaves
falling from the perfect plane trees
which line the walkways.

Autumn Waiting

Crows are waiting
for the train with me;
first they sway on top of
thinning maples, then leaving
a few leaves as reminder
they descend to make
long liquid shadows;
one sits on a black and white
sign perfectly blending,
another disappears
over a new black pick-up;
with a single caw
they announce the arrival on time.

In My Hometown

On a windy winter day
a pair of crows clutched the railing
of our park's reviewing stand.
Talons gripped and grasped the wood
as if to start a race.
Their bodies hunched as if
to debate.
But this was no Mark Twain tale,
no rivalry lurked here
nor dark denouement.
Animal life had taken over
again in simple metaphor.

CROW'S ROLES

Crow is tightrope man
on wires overhead,
master-of-ceremonies
shrugging his shoulders
seeming to laugh down
on turmoil of traffic,
perhaps hoping for jam up
waiting for whirling red lights,
we disturb his world
so he disturbs ours,
he only eats what's
already been killed,
he's no killer.

IN THE AIR

Motes of soot in the air
after a coal train has passed.
Hang-gliders in flight
without fear of
invisible wires that
could cut in two,
to reunite in comic fusion.
Spry old man auditioning
for Phantom of the Opera.
Black dots which if they
continued to fill in
would blot out the picture
entirely.

CORVINE CANVAS

Let's contemplate the sky
to see what crow unconsciously
can create upon it:
with his ability to seem
to stall midway in space,
an impending storm,
his shape a smut on the sky,
reenactment of
aerial bombardment
in persona of flak—
perhaps more amiable
hint of witch's tailcoat
on a frosty eve.

CROWS ABOVE THE ROAD

They come on at dawn
heading east in a tight line
headlights glaring,
blind to all but
the white stripe on the road,
wearing blank black eyes
or eyes afire.
At dusk they are back
heading west into flickers
on the horizon,
feathered backs of heads
or turnips withered after
a season in the cellar.

The Crow

The eye of crow
is a noble shield
a pool of multi-worlds
a convex observation booth
the color of shade, shadow
night and secret places,
his talons grasp loving things
which nourish and are passed on
the sheer of dusky wing
with minuscule adjustment
against wayward winds
against all seasons
he satirizes
contemporary time
by perching on a
a parking meter.

THE CROWS

These good old men
all they need are pince-nez
balanced on their bulbous beaks
as acting gowned academics,
an apt subject for
the Haida to carve
in a song of wisdom.
Husband, provider
father, counselor
crows have been all that,
suitable for mankind
to honor if he
would only look.

WINTER CROWS

More limber than those
wooden ducks,
more laid back than those
nervous geese,
crows always look
significant against
frost-covered ground,
the shadow of their wings
more powerful,
the sound they make
like a challenge from inside
an armored helmet
to anyone passing.

Crow On A Walnut

Turn it to the right
to notice the lacy
grace of the wing.
Shift it to the left
to sense the subtle
arc of the proboscis.
Now place it on a branch
of the old walnut
until it balances there
without a nudge of wind.
Touch it on the head
with human magic to see
how it comes to life.

Watching Crows Watching Me

I often didn't trust crows.
I watched them. They watched me.
I put on sunglasses
so they couldn't see my eyes.
Funny, how eyes don't change
although we do.
Best to disguise the fact.
Then I saw a crow waft up
to the peak of a phone pole
where another crow sat.
The first fed the other something
delicately, lovingly.
Funny, how attitudes change.

CROW

The crow is blacker
than the lowest rain cloud,
blacker than that dirt clod
turned over in a field.
(But he can think
he can talk,
he has performed
evil acts, I am sure,
but comes from
a long line of nobility.)
As the sun breaks through,
his plumage turns as varied
as the brightest abalone.

CROW'S VOICE

Does the crow's
"Caw—caw—caw"
mean "Yes—yes—yes
something is right
below in the grove,"
or does it mean
"No—no—no
a storm is building
there behind the clouds."
Perhaps he just does it
for reassurance
as he flies alone
across a barren place.

ON A POLE

Out of seeming deadness
of a country day
a bare pole stands by the road
stripped of its wires.
A crow lands on top—
scratches beak awhile—
shifts for position—
some random calls for attention—
does a little auctioneering—
spouts a few bromides.
Then stone-like to the ground
he mouths some grub and
wings off to his brood.

CROW COUNTRY

First, crows glide in the air
above the fields like
misplaced punctuation,
their mutterings a curse
on land-bound beings,
or imprecations
at being disturbed.
Then, they become parts of larches—
black leaves, branches stretching
out feathery shadows,
their eye a gleam of insight,
a marble orb which ordains all
that will happen in their realm.

CROWS GONE

I don't see crows anymore,
am I crazy?
they rule the world
they're everywhere
I saw them in China and India.
My buddies
telling yarns
cackling their feathered asses off
their eyes as dodgy as a card shark,
raising families just like
any honest American.
Where are they—
nailed above a cabin door?
Am I blind—
if so I have gained
a pregnant blackness
just like them.

A Dead Crow

Wind is trying to help
some feathers ruffle
but it is no use—
the body flat, eyes gone,
ants reconnoitering;
family moments,
tales told and laughter with friends,
wisdom accumulated,
the cagey strut on
wires and fence posts,
to look down on
and comment upon
the human condition.

The Caw

The caw is from
a hanging birch twisted,
sheared of pestiferous bark;
the caw is of a carcass
waylaid by auto or gun
for sport not venison
to lie rotting, ripe for some;
the caw is about
an abyss
of desolate sandstone walls
that falls and falls
which useless sun scalds—
the caw echoes, echoes.

The Showdown

They closed in,
he was surrounded.
They came out of the shadows
making him their own.
Sneers were on some faces,
masks pulled low,
eyes narrow tar pits.
Not even a whisper
a mumble could be heard.
But he stood his ground
as the crows stared, and
the vulture did not stop
his feasting on the carcass.

The Wings Of Wyeth's Crow

swooped by my window
—black spot in my eye
palsied drooping lid—
I peered again to realize
not a jostling clown
or scheming scavenger
but arrowed and potent;
I heard its talons take
upon the rain gutter
somewhere overhead,
wondering what move next,
yet nothing as if this
magic had evaporated.

CROW MUSIC

Crow lingo is springs spronging
they slump in crow trees yapping,
their staccato rhythms added to
not interrupted,
first topic is always weather
next family
a local bully
though they can be one too—
then of a sudden
they are gone with the sound
of clapping bed sheets
to another venue
undisclosed.

A MURDER OF CROWS

Watch them bask in sun
hold wings open to rain,
one marvelous sport
to catch fluttering in air
cherry blossoms.
Are you disgusted
by crows on the road
gorging on the dead,
yet they stand silently
around their fallen
in humble contemplation.
Do not show your face
for they will remember.

Corvine Games

Crows cling to cornstalks
resembling ears turned
far beyond the season.
On the grass they position
themselves like footballers,
then one shuffles away
with the gait of a kicked dog.
I stop to stare one down
reading in his eyes a chain
of thoughts, till he realizes
it's not worth taking
a chance with such a crazy
human and launches off.

To Crows

As late summer spreads
its longer reflections,
you stretch broad wings over
a season growing soundless.
You are always there cavorting
in the grass, flicking off to
unspoken locations or
grouping in groves to discuss
esoteric things.
You will soon reign over
a desolate winter world,
like local nabobs
dominating their turf.

CROW APPEARANCES

Crow is always appearing
in my life—daring
to invade even
the privacy of my dreams.
I see him among parked cars
along the street in spring tossing
tidbits on the ground, a nut?
a butt? a bit of warm meat?
On a raw winter's day
he is stomping down the snow
to make a flat space
where he can wait—for what!
Do you posture, wearing
a sailor's black turtleneck?
Will you turn so I,
the servant, can take your cloak?

SYMBOLS AS CROWS

Amid the savage
whirlwind loosed on lawns
there they are!
Skirring over
devastation of hard fields
there they are!
Despite how cold can
rigidify our minds
or rattle our souls
there they are!
One crow pumping toward
a cloud on the hill
shows us what we might do.

UBIQUITOUS

Now that the road is closed (or
is it that the corn is in)
crows have invaded
everywhere—
one crow atop each beech
one on every phone pole
a crow per mail box.
Part-buzzard part-eagle
I cannot tell which anymore,
they tidy up all discards
on this forsaken road,
I know who will take over
if we lose our grip.

EVERYWHERE

Have you noticed? crows
are everywhere!
any country you pick.
they coast down streets like hang-gliders,
they perch in untoward niches
like narks taking notes.
A call from an ivy wall—
it's a crow its yellow beak
a flower of discovery.
Humans are still trying
to communicate,
but snap an invisible
finger and crow squadrons descend.

CROW DAY

Breezy spring at sixty-five degrees,
crows swing on wires
letting wind blow through
their feathers till they
resemble Daffy Duck;
one on a stump, other
somewhere in the woods
they call arcanely,
shaving by windshields
to let drivers know;
as dusk tighten the blinds
their catcalls drown out
songs of dove and owl.

CROW TREES

Glare in the sky,
shadows blot branches
even drip-drop days,
raggedy wings flap
making their own fruit,
hanging out gray laundry;
everybody's watchmen
everybody's nuisance
their ever jostling
their casual lingo
echo down the streets,
they own the neighborhood
in the sky.

CROW TREE

This morning family men
swaying on branches
shifting back & forth,
spinning a lot of corny ones
telling the kid a thing or two
borrowing a few from the Mrs.
Later the classic joker
sneering and jeering
at the farmers below
or the sandlot baseball game,
ready to dodge the flung stone
with a raucous flap
then back with the eternal heckle.

COME TO EARTH

The sky is a stew
stirred with cloud grays and sky
blues,
as crows drop like pieces of oil
cloth onto the ground.
Preposterously they stump
around like men in rubber
flippers finding the land
they knew so well suddenly
difficult to navigate.
They don't talk, they know their job
they leave, all except one
who is ready for
dive-bombing grackles.

CROWS RULE THE WORLD

They are guardians on the gates
of old estates.
Their shadows draw you in.
Their voices are
diabolic tittering
blessed by witches.
Do not try to follow
for they turn to white
in the sky
and hide behind the moon.
There are uncertainties overhead.
Even if you run home to hide
they are blackness in your bed.

.

WIRED

Crow comments on The 12 Days of
Xmas:
So **SWANS CAN SWIM**?
big deal
FRENCH HENS
hell, we're everywhere in the world
Come off it, **TURTLE DOVES**
cooing is a private matter
CALLING BIRDS means they're
caught in cages,
there ought to be a law!
A **PARTRIDGE**, pheasant, grouse,
whatever—
they're all sitting ducks!
GEESE LAYING is no great trick—
try dodging a back-hoe in a cornfield!

Six Crows For Christmas

Six crows slipping on
the sleety sidewalk,
balancing on the curb
as the gutter gushes,
flicking flakes from their backs
impervious to windy eyes,
picking up and discarding
among leftovers on the block,
to search for tokens
for what we cannot fathom,
five crows for Christmas
one timid beside a bush
the rest bold in the world.

Proselytizing

As they flutter out from the church
don't be surprised by crows' robes,
they are great glad-handers
cawing all earthly delights,
then have you repenting
signing on the dotted line.
They leave the cassocks
in the loft for bats,
then scour the land until
they find you tortured
in your chamber when
their passing shadow
hints that there is hope.

Fox And Crow

From the tops of spruce
crows toss around balls of calls.
A crow imitates
a baby crying,
then a man under-
water gurgling.
Fox looks up bewildered
turns her muff in a huff,
knowing she can't sell
anything here, not
even one grape.
A very ripe piece of fruit
is crow clasped to a cornstalk.

A Grape's Worth

Crows have been nibbling
at the grapes again,
they try to take off like
overloaded cargo planes,
they hang upside down
on limbs like chickadees
until gravity claims them.
They are shaped by weather,
cold days hunching near
the silo mumbling rumor,
but blue-straw-rasp-berries
don't have that special kick
as days of grape languor.

GARGOYLE

O, crow, you are the modern
answer to gargoyles.
Head and wing burned black
for your constancy,
you are a chimera
of multiple moods.
You cling to a corbel
and peer down as either
guardian to good
or warning against evil.
At night you surge over
to survey the cafes and
perhaps dare a sip of the vine.

CROWS LIKE HISTORY

Crows like history,
have you ever noticed?
Their dry calls often
come out of old hickories
as if they were hawkers
on Fourth Avenue
selling ancient tomes.
Likewise, on the highway
they pick through the leavings
to find bones and measure
the worth of their whiteness.
Crows too are as old as
any redwoods around.

The Book Of Nature

A book to me is nature,
holding leaves within it,
bound in ancient hide
which could just as well be bark;
wild things like crows in
a naked beech as
left over decorations,
without wind the flock
blowing over a field
which looks like rent cloth;
as I read aloud, the book
grows leaves which fly up, and
a ghost flickers in my throat.

Corvine Chess

Crows spread out over the grass
to play living chess.
Largest crow is king,
queen ubiquitous.
Black knight proves apt title,
in black the bishops
become satanic.
Instead of castles which crows
have clamped on for centuries,
rooks are their cousins.
Arranging its stars as pawns
by nightfall the moon has laid
a chessboard cross the lake.

CROWS UNDER TREES

One crow stands under sycamores.
If it were another bird
I wouldn't have noticed.
But the crow is so large,
his feathers so black
like a man whose sole wealth
is the coat wrapped round him.
I turn to a book
on Superstition
to find that crows can be men
lost under a spell—
yes, I can understand that.
Also, crows have the power
to bury some treasure.
The poplars where the crow stands
appear hulking and dark
with the ground beneath
somehow funereal bare.
I'll wait here to see
if the crow digs up something.

In The Home

Gilt epaulet on my shoulder,
no, too solid and showy.
Crow on my shoulder
tries out his wings as
a weight-lifter would flex his pecs.
I move carefully
offering him an ort,
getting him to stay
to whisper the secret
in my ear.
With a sudden bustle
they push my wheelchair
down the corridor.

Crawan Tactics

One crow utters
the 4-caw alert,
a crow starts the bulldozer
and topples it in-
to a foundation.
A female crow (they're smarter)
puts the dump truck into
reverse and crashes
it over the ravine.
Cornfields have been here
for over a hundred years
and crows demand to know
where the corn has gone!

The Raven's Eye

The raven's eye
makes the sun
makes the world
makes the perfect pond.
In his eye is the whirlpool
the crest flashing,
his intelligence
his creativity
his imagination.
Which allows us to live
in his eye,
he is the taker of life
he is the great giver.

Raving

A raven of an idea
lighted on my shoulder,
gravelly whispered from
under a Chaplin mustache.
A true tout he assured me
he wasn't talking women this time,
he wouldn't be cryptic.
It was simple, he said,
it was a sure thing
right in front of you
the meaning to life is . . .
But now an onyx bust stood
before me, my shoulders lightened.

An Unkindness Of Ravens

They play at hopscotch
but want nothing to do
with children in the park,
they play castanets
but don't wish to associate
with Spanish ladies.
Their wings in furbelows
they prefer to be
black antimacassars in
a dark house, from where they mass
against a dusky sky
preening in the mirror of moon,
then glide home to family.

In Cap And Cape

In dark cap and cape
a crucifix of crows
clutches a bare locust
about to hoarsely croak
down its decision.
On a desolate snowfield
a coven of crows
stands in a broken circle
about to cast a spell
the countryside will long remember.
Dim light, wind beyond,
the crows of dusk
fill the valley.

Meditation On A Crow

The ashen cloud
that scuds over
is etched with inlets and coves.
I concentrate on
what is not there in the cedar.
It's as difficult
to predict the past
as it is in a smoky globe.
Something sticks in my mind
and will not evaporate.
Crow speaks perfect
iambic tetrameter.
Then he is gone.

Four Crows

Under a sky flattened
by slate clouds, four crows
grip a hemlock tree.
Soft pliant boughs making
perfect seats, I half
expect them to
carom the pool balls.
They speak to each other
as through trumpet mouthpieces.
They look over shoulders
down at me, look again then
shear away with a curse to
another murky billiard hall.

Trickster

Raven bounced across the grass
in his pantaloons and ruff
dragging his hobo sack.
He pulled out his tricks
rolling in the snow,
flying toward gunshots,
hiding others' food
but forgetting where.
He winked with his good eye
at all who caught him.
When he got home
he took off his mask
to reveal crow.

Liberal Arts

Crow gargles like
a strangling man,
then vibrantly clacks his beak
like Siamese sticks.
His caws and posings
rate impeccable,
complete mystery
his cornfield actions.
Music and theater
are woven through crow's life,
in addition to
painting sunset landscapes
with a blue-black brush.

Crow's Moods

In the daytime
crow clicks oyster shells,
he dances along a rail fence
watching us go by.
Crows huddle on the lawn
deciding
to take positions to perform
their own minuet.
In the middle of the night
crow calls from a vale,
he warbles from a swamp
keens from a cemetery,
this is all we can hear.

Sentry Crow

In early morning air
after brown fog dissolves,
a crow hoots and hoots
never breaking rhythm
while a human wants to flee.
On a branch the crow scratches
his beak and opens it
to take a sniff like
an old man asking, "Eh?"
Then a second crow lands
on a nearby cedar
and they say nothing
till the first goes off duty.

ONLY ACTING

Hanging out by the tracks
in an old chesterfield
looking for a spud or two.
But what a head of hair
coal-black waving in the wind,
and glowing white teeth.
With his cronies he chortles
in sleet or humidity,
even there at nightfall
when ruts gleam in moonlight.
And yet at anytime
wiping off his make-up
he can rise and scoot.

CROWS ENDURE

Against evergreen woods
crows hover darkly then
on a slight angle
turn blue-black in sun sheer;
they perch ungainly
on a stalk resembling
swaying ears of corn;
overall it is they
who have overshadowed
all other birds in size
and decibels of hooting;
so let them be major actors
in this landscape.

Into Crow

I've always wanted to
balance this lightly on a branch.
I raise one arm,
a feathered shadow
appears on the ground.
Eyesight has never been so clear,
I can see each twitch
in the meadow below.
I sense weather now as
well as ABC,
have family,
I sit here comfortably bare,
a new life.

About the Author

Ray Greenblatt has written twenty books of poetry in his fifty years of writing. He is presently an editor on the *Schuylkill Valley Journal* and teaches a Joy of Poetry course in its ninth year at OLLI-Temple University. He was on the board of the Philadelphia Writers Conference and spoke at the John Steinbeck Festival in Salinas, California. Lately, he has been diversifying by writing book reviews for the John Updike Society, Dylan Thomas Society, and the Graham Greene Society.

His earlier publications include: *Just Beyond Maracaibo; A Windfall of Rivers; February Always Happens; To Find the Winterbourn; Puzzles in the Woods; Strange Forest of Words; Dvorak's Garage; Inside the Kuiper Belt; Bleached Spines;* and *Shadow with Green Eyes.*

Ray Greenblatt lives in Wayne, PA and Charlestown, MD (but not simultaneously).

Colophon

This book is set in several weights and variants of Adobe Brioso Pro, designed by master calligrapher and type designer Robert Slimbach, modeled on his formal roman and italic script.

The words on the cover are hand-lettered by Meg Kennedy, in a style designed by Ben Shahn.

9 780979 586163